BILL EVANS / the 70's

B MINOR WALTZ 3
("You Must Believe In Spring" — Warner Bros. lp HS-3504)

FOR NENETTE 14
("New Conversations" — Warner Bros. lp BSK-3177)

LAURIE 16
("We Will Meet Again" — Warner Bros. lp HS-3411;
"The Paris Concert — Edition Two" — Elektra Musician lp 60311-1-E)

MAXINE 10
("New Conversations" — Warner Bros. lp BSK-3177)

REMEMBERING THE RAIN 13
("New Conversations" — Warner Bros. lp BSK-3177)

SONG FOR HELEN 8
("New Conversations" — Warner Bros. lp BSK-3177)

WE WILL MEET AGAIN 18
("We Will Meet Again" — Warner Bros. lp HS-3411;
"You Must Believe In Spring" — Warner Bros. lp HS-3504)

YOUR STORY 22
("Bill Evans — A Tribute" — Palo Alto lp PA 8028-2)

Ludlow Music, Inc.

7777 W. BLUEMOUND RD. P.O. BOX 13819 MILWAUKEE, WI 53213

I believe in things that are developed through hard work. I always like people who have developed long and hard, especially through introspection and a lot of dedication. I think what they arrive at is usually a much deeper and more beautiful thing than the person who seems to have that ability and fluidity from the beginning. I say this because it's a good message to give to young talents who feel as I used to.

— Bill Evans,
excerpted from *Contemporary Keyboard*, January 1981

CREDITS:
Piano arrangements: Art Murphy
Cover art: Studio T
Editor: Judy Bell

B MINOR WALTZ

by BILL EVANS

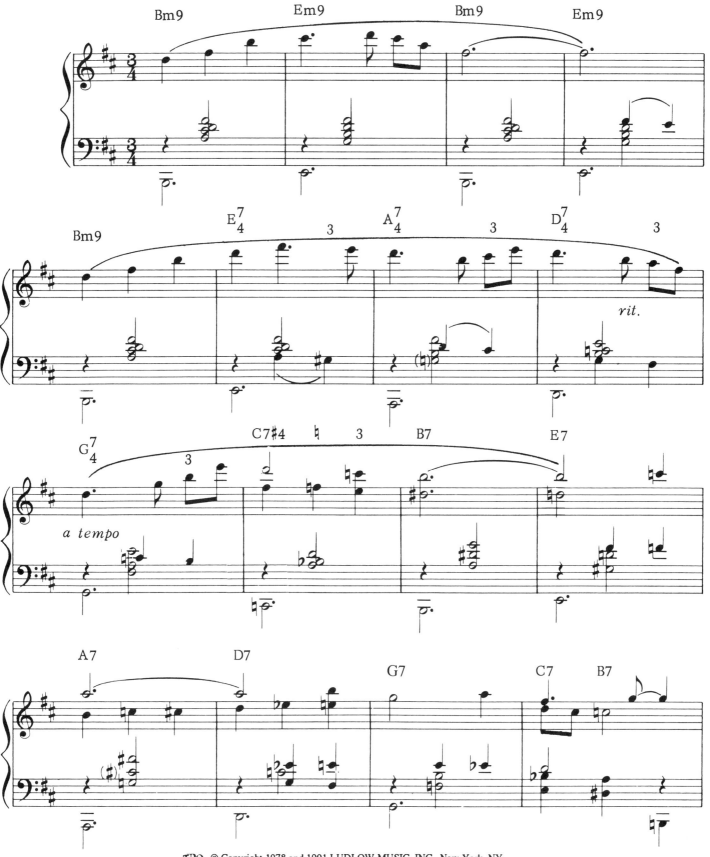

TRO © Copyright 1978 and 1991 LUDLOW MUSIC, INC., New York, NY
International Copyright Secured   Made in U.S.A.
All Rights Reserved Including Public Performance For Profit

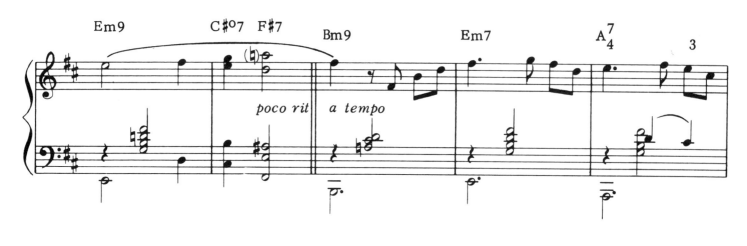

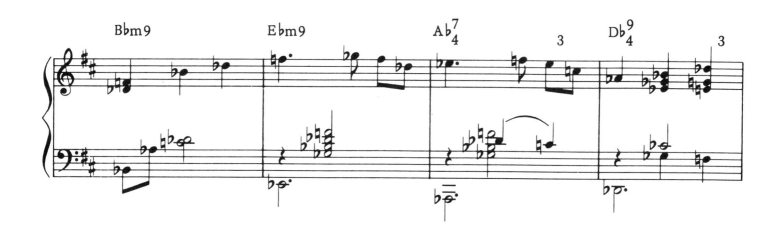
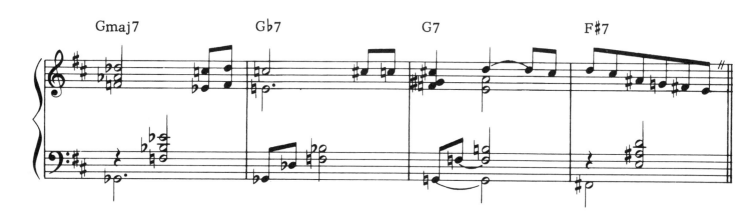

SONG FOR HELEN

by BILL EVANS

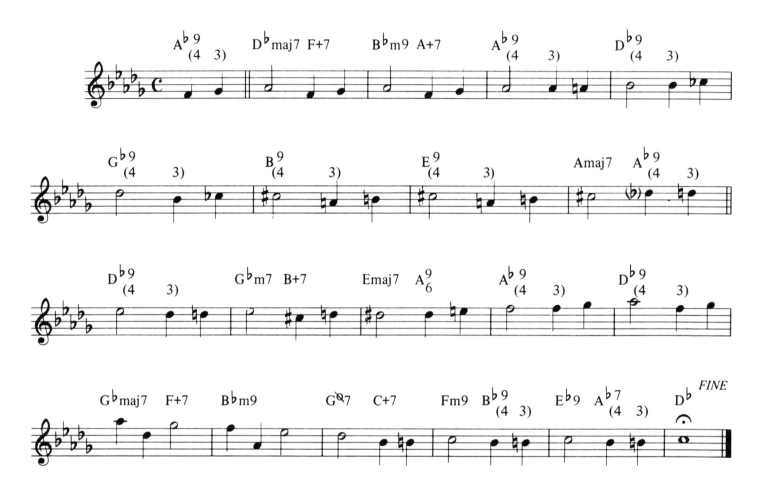

SONG FOR HELEN

by BILL EVANS

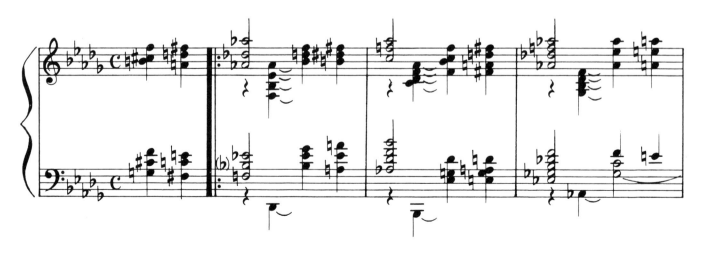

TRO © Copyright 1978 and 1991 LUDLOW MUSIC, INC., New York, NY
International Copyright Secured   Made in U.S.A.
All Rights Reserved Including Public Performance For Profit

MAXINE

by BILL EVANS

REMEMBERING THE RAIN

by BILL EVANS

FOR NENETTE

by BILL EVANS

LAURIE

by BILL EVANS

WE WILL MEET AGAIN

by BILL EVANS

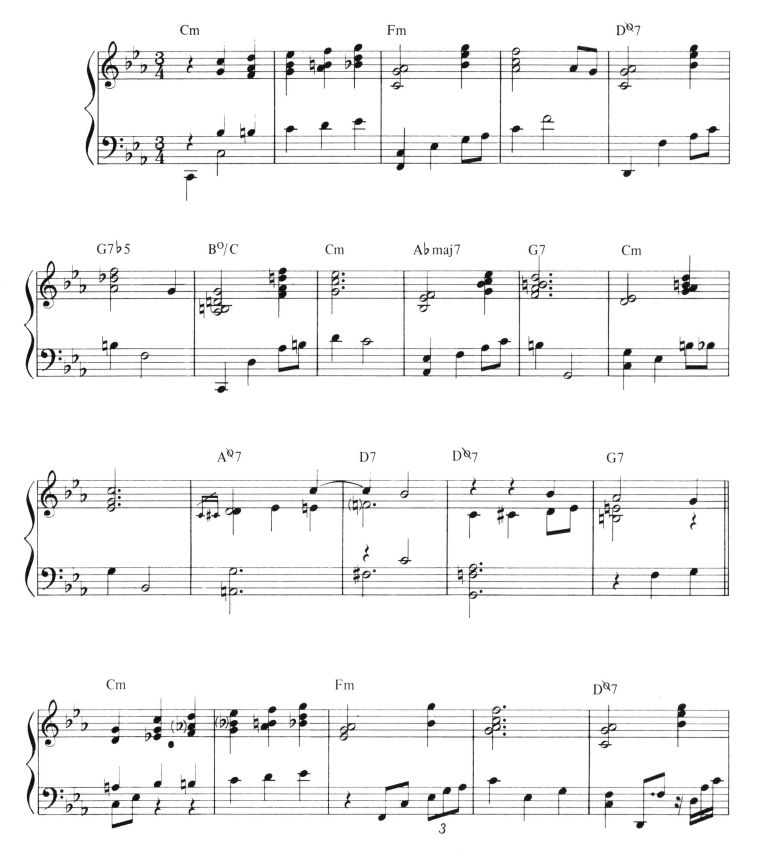

TRO © Copyright 1979 and 1991 LUDLOW MUSIC, INC., New York, NY
International Copyright Secured   Made in U.S.A.
All Rights Reserved Including Public Performance For Profit

* Repeat chord cycle.

YOUR STORY

by BILL EVANS